ON THE HARDWOOD

LOS ANGELES
CLIPPERS

JOSH ANDERSON

On the Hardwood: Los Angeles Clippers

MVP Books
2255 Calle Clara
La Jolla, CA 92037

MVP Books is an imprint of Book Buddy Digital Media, Inc., 42982 Osgood Road, Fremont, CA 94539

MVP Books publications may be purchased for
educational, business, or sales promotional use.

Cover and layout design by Jana Ramsay
Copyedited by Susan Sylvia
Photos by Getty Images

ISBN: 978-1-61570-511-5 (Library Binding)
ISBN: 978-1-61570-510-8 (Soft Cover)

TABLE OF CONTENTS

Chapter 1
WELCOME TO LOB CITY

There was no better voice to describe the dynamic action in the STAPLES Center that evening than Ralph Lawler. Behind the microphone for more than 2,500 Los Angeles Clippers games, Ralph had seen nearly every moment in the franchise's history. Even though it was a meaningless exhibition game as far as standings were concerned, the night had a special feel to it.

Late in the third quarter, the Clippers held a six-point lead and looked to be on the way to a second-straight exhibition victory over the Los Angeles Lakers. In a few nights, the 2011-12 NBA season would begin. If the feeling that evening held true, the packed STAPLES Center might be witnessing the

dawning of a new era in Los Angeles basketball.

Lakers forward Matt Barnes tossed an inbounds pass to his right. Clippers guard Chauncey Billups leapt into the air, nearly leaving his sneakers on the court.

"INBOUNDS PASS, STOLEN BY BILLUPS…"

Falling out of bounds, near the row of photographers kneeling at the Lakers' basket, Billups flipped the ball behind him to save the possession. He found center DeAndre Jordan, who quickly looked up the court and passed to Chris Paul.

"LOOK OUT. HERE COME THE CLIPPERS…"

In the blink of an eye, Paul was into the frontcourt and inside the three-point arc. There was one Laker defender between him and the basket. If he took it to the rim himself, he had a decent chance for two points. But then, as if out of nowhere, a better-than-decent option appeared to Paul's left.

"HERE COMES GRIFFIN…"

Paul picked up his dribble with his right hand, scooped the ball into the air over the Laker defender, but short of the basket.

Starting his leap just inside of the free-throw line, Blake Griffin elevated toward the ball. He leaped, unconcerned with who might be in his way, reached out with both hands and grabbed the ball. He soared to the hoop.

"SLAM DUNK!"

As Griffin flushed the ball through the basket, the crowd went bananas for this playoff atmosphere in the preseason. For the

Chris Paul dribbles past Metta World Peace of the Lakers.

Clippers' faithful, this preseason sweep of the rival Lakers signaled the dawning of a new era in Los Angeles basketball.

Sure, it was only preseason, but for the Clippers to decisively outplay the Lakers was a big deal. The Clips had also clearly established an identity that was very different from this Lakers team. The Lakers had won two of the last three NBA titles and had plenty of experience. But this Clippers team was more athletic, more dynamic. Hungrier for the glory of a championship, possibly.

The two preseason wins over the Lakers gave everyone reason to believe in the possibility of a future where the Clippers were the hot ticket in town, and NBA Championship contenders.

Griffin dunks over the Lakers' Pau Gasol.

Even the most loyal Los Angeles Clippers fan will admit that, for most of the franchise's history, their team has rightfully earned the title of "L.A.'s Other Team." While the Lakers have piled up conference championships and NBA titles, the Clippers have averaged only one winning season out of every five in their 40-plus years in the league.

Everything changed—or, at least, it looked like it might *start* to change—in December of 2011. NBA owners and players had finally resolved the issues that resulted in a lockout. The NBA season was going to start late, but fans, owners, and players were happy. Basketball was right around the corner.

Although they missed the playoffs for the fifth straight season,

the Clippers had been one of the league's most promising young teams in the 2010-11 season. Rookie of the Year Blake Griffin had proven himself to be one of the best power forwards in the league. And, to the delight of Clippers fans, he was one of the most exciting and dynamic dunkers in the NBA.

In addition to Griffin, the Clippers had young center DeAndre Jordan, and a young, athletic backcourt. Even though it was generally agreed that they were not a title contender yet, most journalists covering the league felt that the young Clippers would contend for a playoff spot once the league resumed play for 2011-12.

A few weeks before the season began, it looked like the Clippers would again have to sit on the sidelines while the Lakers made a move to put them in title contention. The Lakers were very close to completing a three-way trade with the New Orleans Hornets and Houston Rockets to acquire Chris Paul.

Paul's credentials through seven NBA seasons are nothing short of groundbreaking: 2005-06 Rookie of the Year, five straight All-Star appearances, five-time NBA steals leader. Perhaps most striking is that the young point guard ranks third in

DeAndre Jordan, the Clippers' young center, goes up for a dunk.

A Haul for Paul

The Clippers sent Eric Gordon, Chris Kaman, Al-Farouq Aminu, and a first-round draft pick to the New Orleans Hornets in return for Chris Paul.

NBA history in assists-per-game.

With Paul, the Lakers would have had a star to team with Kobe Bryant for the next few years, and then take the stage as the Lakers' centerpiece for the foreseeable future.

Hours after the trade was announced, though, the deal fell apart. Suddenly, the Clippers were back in the mix for Chris Paul.

A few days later, in the midst of preparing for the upcoming season, several Clippers were gathered for a league outreach event at a Los Angeles school. DeAndre Jordan received a text message from his agent that said, "Great trade."

Jordan called his agent and asked what had happened. As he heard the news he gestured for his teammate, Griffin, to come over. When

Griffin, seen here at a community outreach event, coined the team's nickname, "Lob City."

Jordan shared the news that Paul was joining the Clippers, the frontcourt-mates did a chest bump. It was only appropriate that it was Griffin who first uttered the term that would become the Clippers' new nickname.

"Yeah!!!," Griffin announced. "It's going to be Lob City!!"

With a little more than a week before games began, an already hopeful season took on another level of excitement. They wouldn't have much practice time together, but based on the talent on their roster, the Clippers looked like genuine contenders. Instead of quietly hoping the team would earn a spot in the playoffs, fans would now loudly demand it.

Everyone knew the addition of Chris Paul would bring a lot of alley-oops, dunks, and plenty more exciting scoring opportunities. But, the question the Clippers needed to answer, coming into the 2011-12 season, was whether "Lob City" could win over Los Angeles from the Lakers. The only way to do that would be to compete for the NBA's greatest prize: the Larry O'Brien Trophy.

Chris Paul, seen here holding up his new jersey, ranks third in NBA history in assists-per-game!

Chapter 2
A Team on the Move

The Clippers started their time in the NBA about as far from the beaches of Southern California as you can get: Buffalo, New York.

The Buffalo Braves joined the league for the 1970-71 season as an expansion franchise. They played eight seasons in upstate New York, and reached the NBA playoffs three times. Not bad, but they were knocked out in the first round twice, and the second round once.

Although their success as a team was limited during their time in Buffalo, the Braves did boast one of the league's best players during this time, Bob McAdoo.

McAdoo was unique for a man who played in the 1970s. Most players his size—6'9", or larger—played the more typical back-to-the-basket,

post-up style at that time. McAdoo, though, was just as skilled hitting a long jumper as he was battling close to the rim. His averages of 34.5 points per game and 14.1 rebounds per

Buffalo Braves player Bob McAdoo was one of the best players of the early '70s.

game earned him the Most Valuable Player award in 1975.

McAdoo is one of four Hall of Famers to play for the Braves/Clippers franchise during his career, and the only player to win an MVP as a member of the team.

After two straight losing seasons resulted in low attendance in Buffalo, the team moved across the country to San Diego in 1978. After a contest to name the team, the name Clippers was chosen, after the large sailing ships that sometimes pass through San Diego Bay.

The Clippers' time in San Diego started out well enough. The team posted a 43-39 record in 1978-79. But the success would stop there.

The 1979-80 season would be the first of 12 straight losing years, encompassing the entire decade of the 1980s. Again, poor play on the court resulted in low attendance at Clippers games. The team was sold during this time, and moved north to Los Angeles, in hopes that a larger city would mean more fans would come

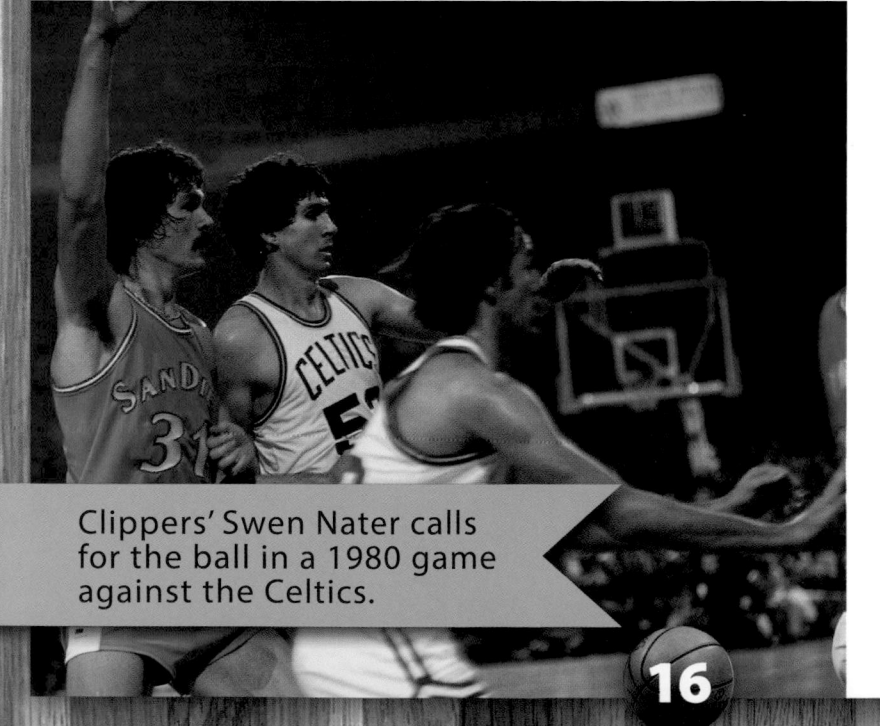

Clippers' Swen Nater calls for the ball in a 1980 game against the Celtics.

to the games.

While the Clippers had some very exciting players during 1980s, such as World B. Free, Norm Nixon, and Bill Walton, they never appeared in the playoffs. Furthermore, the team sent only three representatives to the All-Star Game that decade.

By virtue of their poor finish during the 1987-88 season, the Clippers earned the first pick in the 1988 NBA Draft. This gave them the opportunity to draft one of the most accomplished college basketball players in history.

During his time at the University of Kansas, Danny Manning led the Jayhawks to the Final Four twice. In 1988, his Jayhawks won the National Championship, and Manning was named the College Player of the Year

Kansas's Danny Manning, 1988 College Player of the Year, was the Clippers' first pick.

and the Most Outstanding Player of the Final Four.

When the Clippers made Manning the first pick in the draft, it marked a ray of hope for the franchise. Could Manning do for

Back to Kansas

After his playing career ended, Danny Manning spent nine years on the coaching staff at the University of Kansas.

Dr. Jack

Dr. Jack Ramsay, who coached the Buffalo Braves from 1972 to 1976, was elected to the Naismith Memorial Basketball Hall of Fame in 1992.

the Clippers what he had done for the Jayhawks? Fans, executives, and teammates hoped so.

In 1991-92, Manning led the Clippers to their first playoff

Danny Manning eyes an opening in a 1992 game against the Denver Nuggets.

appearance since their early years in Buffalo. The Clippers were set to play the Utah Jazz, and weren't thought to have much of a chance in the series. While most fans and media following the league might've predicted a sweep, the Clippers hadn't waited this long to go away quietly—even if they were matched up against future Hall of Famers, John Stockton and Karl Malone.

The Jazz took the first two games of the series in Utah. But the Clippers battled to a victory in Los Angeles in Game 3. Then, due to the L.A. riots associated with the verdict in the famed Rodney King trial, Game 4 was moved to Anaheim.

Despite the change in location, the Clippers prevailed in Game 4, then headed to Utah for a decisive

Game 5. The Jazz's Hall-of-Fame combo was too much for the Clips, though, and L.A. bowed out of the playoffs after the exciting first-round series.

The Clippers would be right back in the same position the next year, pushing the heavily favored Houston Rockets to a fifth game in their first-round series. Houston's legendary center Hakeem Olajuwon was too much for the Clippers in Game 5, though, and the Rockets won the series.

These two playoff seasons would mark one of the great highlights in franchise history. After the 1992-93 season, the Clippers would go on to finish with a losing record in each of the next twelve years.

Danny Manning and Ron Harper try to stop the Rockets' Hakeem Olajuwon.

Despite missing the playoffs and finishing with only 37 wins during the 2004-05 season, the Clippers could take heart in the fact that they finished with a better record than the Lakers.

Generally, one mediocre team finishing ahead of another isn't worthy of celebrating, but the Clippers hadn't outshined the Lakers in the standings since 1993!

The Clippers had spent the late 1990s and the early 2000s trying to build a team that could compete with the top teams in the league. But, several strokes of bad luck during this time slowed the rebuilding process, including disappointments and injuries to high draft picks.

Coming into the 2005-06 season, an optimistic fan could look at the

Blue Devils Wearing Red
The 2005-06 Clippers had three former Duke Blue Devils on the roster: Elton Brand, Corey Maggette, and Daniel Ewing.

roster and see a lot of potential. Elton Brand was one of the best forwards in the league, capable of a 20-point, 10-rebound performance nearly every night. Former NBA champion Sam Cassell had been acquired to provide veteran leadership at the point guard position. And youngsters Chris Kaman and Shaun Livingston had both shown great potential the season before, leading some to think each could develop into a star.

The well-rounded Clippers started the 2005-06 season on a tear. They won 14 of their first 20 games, including a 102-90 victory over

Elton Brand was one of the best forwards in the league in 2005-06.

LeBron James' Cleveland Cavaliers. The team finished with 45 wins, the most for the team since their years in Buffalo. Elton Brand had the best season for a Clipper in recent history, averaging almost 25 points per

A Valuable Brand

When Elton Brand made the All-Star Team in 2002, he was the first Clipper to do so since Danny Manning in 1994.

game, 10 rebounds, and 2.5 blocked shots.

Their first-round playoff matchup was a tough one against the Denver Nuggets. Although the Clippers had won more games, the Nuggets won their division. The Nuggets had one of the few scorers who outdid Elton Brand that season in second-year forward Carmelo Anthony.

In Game 1 of the series with the Nuggets, in front of a screaming crowd at the STAPLES Center, the Clippers got their first playoff win in 13 years. Sam Cassell led the way with 19 points and seven assists. The Clippers took the second game as well, 98-87, and put themselves in a good position with the series going back to Denver.

After losing Game 3, Corey

Maggette, who had missed much of the year with an injury, scored 19 points in Game 4 and left the Clippers one win away from their first series victory since their Buffalo days.

Game 5 was back in Los Angeles and the Clippers won by 18. They'd finally won a playoff series and all of a sudden looked like a team with the firepower to contend for a championship.

The Clippers would now face the Phoenix Suns. The winner of the series would go on to the Western Conference Finals. The Suns were led by dynamic point guard Steve Nash and high-flying forward Shawn Marion.

The teams split the first six games, each winning three. The franchise was one game from the Conference Finals—uncharted territory for the Clippers. But to make it there, they'd have to win Game 7 on the road.

Corey Maggette came up big in the 2006 NBA Playoffs against Denver.

The Clippers came close, but the Suns prevailed in Game 7.

The Suns had been to the playoffs regularly with the players on their current roster and simply had too much playoff experience, and too much firepower, for the upstart Clippers. The Suns took Game 7 127-107 and ended what had been a dream season for Clippers fans.

After the season, Elton Brand was named All-NBA Second Team. The franchise was headed in the right direction. The 2005-06 season is widely considered the most successful in franchise history.

Even though that season was a wonderful ride for everyone in-volved with the team, it was followed by five straight losing years, including a terrible 19-win season in 2008-09. Promising young point guard Shaun Livingston was lost during this stretch to a devastating injury.

The good news, however, is that the Clippers' luck in the NBA Draft looked to be changing. While many years had passed with the Clippers having little to show for their poor finishes, help was on the way.

Few number-one picks in the NBA Draft had turned out as disappointingly as the Clippers' choice of Michael Olowokandi in 1998. The Clippers got another chance with the top pick 11 years later in 2009, and the result would be dramatically different. Eventually. But not

before another stroke of bad luck that looked like it might hobble the franchise for years to come.

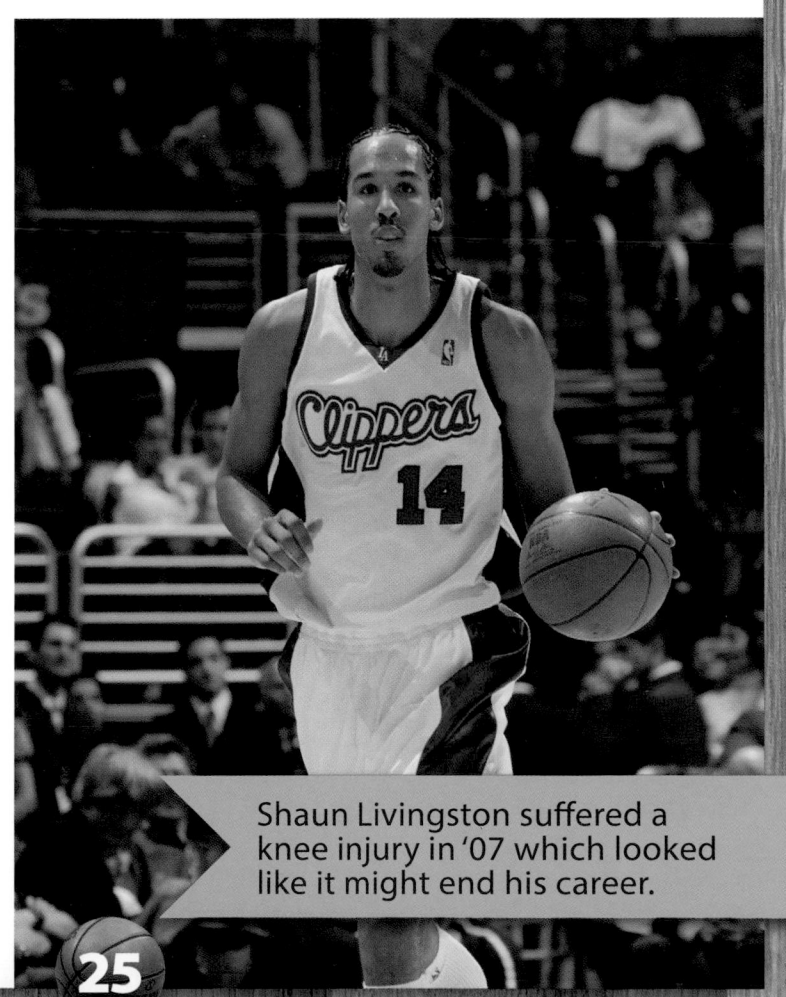

Shaun Livingston suffered a knee injury in '07 which looked like it might end his career.

One player can change the history of a basketball team. Imagine the Bulls without Michael Jordan, the Spurs without Tim Duncan, or the Heat without Dwyane Wade. All of those players came to their teams as high picks in the NBA Draft.

The order in which teams select players is determined by the Draft Lottery, which takes place during the playoffs.

At the Draft Lottery, every team that missed the playoffs the season before has their name placed on a certain number of ping-pong balls. The balls are then put in a large machine. Teams with more losses during that season get more ping-pong balls. Then, the balls are picked randomly from the machine (meaning each ball has an equal

Heads or Tails?
Before the Draft Lottery started in 1985, the first pick was decided by a coin flip between the two worst teams.

chance of being chosen) for the first, second, and third picks in the NBA Draft. This means that every non-playoff team gets a chance at the top picks.

The NBA lottery machine.

The 2008-09 season was another disappointing one for the Clippers. The team finished 19-63—their worst record since 1999-2000. They had some promising young players like DeAndre Jordan and Eric Gordon, but nowhere near enough talent to expect to compete for a playoff spot anytime soon.

Because they had the second-worst record in the league, the Clippers had a lot of ping-pong balls in the machine, which gave them a strong chance of receiving an early pick.

Although there's no guarantee of success in the NBA, every team dreams of getting the lucky ping-pong ball for the top pick in the draft. Coming into 2009, the Clippers had won

The Clippers chose Eric Gordon with the seventh pick in the 2008 NBA Draft.

the Lottery twice. In 1988, they picked Danny Manning, who became a cornerstone of the franchise for six seasons, and led the Clippers to the play-offs twice. In 1998, they took Michael Olowokandi with the first pick—ahead of players like Vince Carter, Dirk Nowitzki, and Paul Pierce.

As the picks were announced at the 2009 Draft Lottery, starting with the 14th pick and working back toward the first, Clippers fans held their breath. Finally, it was down to two teams for the first pick. Clippers Nation rejoiced when they learned that their team would pick first in the 2009 NBA Draft. And, there was little doubt as to who the pick would be.

Griffin's jersey started popping up everywhere as fans swarmed to wear number 32.

Blake Griffin, a power forward at Oklahoma, had dominated college basketball in 2008-09. Griffin, a sophomore, averaged nearly 23 points and 14 rebounds, and hit on almost 65 percent of his shots. He won all six national Player of the Year awards, and led the Sooners to the Elite Eight in the NCAA

Blake Griffin throws it down as a member of the Oklahoma Sooners.

Tournament for only the eighth time in school history.

Some years, it's a mystery who will be selected with the top pick in the draft. Other years, there's no mystery. "I knew that was Blake," said Mike Dunleavy, the Clippers coach at the time. "No question."

A few weeks later, the Clippers made it official, and NBA Commissioner David Stern began the draft by announcing that Blake Griffin was headed to L.A. With the pick, the Clippers hoped they'd have an anchor for the franchise for many years to come.

Clippers fans came into the 2009-10 season with more reason for excitement than they'd had for several years. But, in the Clippers' final preseason game, another stroke of bad luck would put a damper on all of the excitement of Griffin's arrival.

Griffin headed into the lane and took a pass from guard Sebastian Telfair. Griffin elevated, threw the ball behind his head and slammed home a monster dunk with his right hand. But, when he landed, it was clear something was wrong.

No one realized that night that the broken kneecap Blake Griffin suffered would end his rookie season before it officially began. Griffin was expected to return at some point during the season, but ultimately needed surgery to repair the damage.

Without their first round pick, and with many of the same faces around as the season before, the

Double Trouble

Blake Griffin's brother, Taylor, was also picked in the 2009 NBA Draft, by the Phoenix Suns.

Clippers struggled again in 2009-10, winning only 29 games. The team had improved, but still ranked among the league's worst.

Griffin watches the season opening game against the Lakers in 2009.

Griffin struggled too, trying to keep a positive outlook on his recovery, and his NBA career. "After a while, it was like, 'This is horrible,'" Griffin said of his mindset during his rehabilitation. "There were plenty of times I didn't want to necessarily be there. It was rough. Some days were bad, worse than others… I tried to control it as much as possible and be aware of it."

A little more than a year after the injury, Griffin finally took the court in an official NBA game. Although the Clippers lost by 10 to the Blazers, Griffin shined. He scored 20 points, had 14 rebounds, and showed fans a little bit of what they could get used to in the coming years.

Griffin's first points in the NBA came in a fitting way: About three minutes into his first game, running down the court on a fast break, Clippers' guard Randy Foye spotted Griffin and scooped the ball up underhand toward the rim. Griffin flew through the lane, soared to the ball, and threw down a thunderous jam.

It was almost poetic. The man who would coin the phrase "Lob City," and make so many amazing dunks in the years ahead, began his career at the STAPLES Center by flushing a gorgeous alley-oop.

Griffin was everything the team could've hoped for in his rookie year: He averaged 22 points and

12 rebounds, won NBA Rookie of the Year, and played in the All-Star Game. He even jumped over a car in the Slam Dunk Contest!

The Clippers, though, would struggle again, winning only 32 games. As the 2010-11 season ended, though, there was plenty of hope in Clipper-land. And with the acquisition of Chris Paul right before the 2011-12 season, nearly every fan expected a major improvement in the year ahead.

Blake Griffin slams home another two points!

Chapter 5
A New Era in L.A.

The 2011-12 Clippers' roster looked like one of the best in the NBA. Behind All-Stars Griffin and Paul, they had a talented group eager to taste the playoffs for the first time since 2006.

Head coach Vinny Del Negro was used to making the playoffs and didn't expect to be disappointed in 2011-12. During his playing career, his teams had made the playoffs seven times. And he'd made the playoffs in his first two seasons as a head coach with the Chicago Bulls.

Before the season started, the Clippers needed to re-sign one of their brightest young talents.

If it's possible for a 6'11" high-flying center to sneak up on people, DeAndre Jordan sort of snuck up on the NBA. He improved in each of

A (Very) Brief Stay

In 2001, Vinny Del Negro was traded to the Clippers. But he never played a game for L.A., retiring before the season began.

his first three seasons, and earned a contract extension from the Clippers after the 2010-11 season. In 2011-12, Jordan was second in the NBA with 135 blocked shots.

Head coach Vinny Del Negro and Chris Paul talk strategy.

DeAndre Jordan goes up for the block against Tim Duncan.

free agent addition to the Clippers. He brought toughness and perimeter scoring to the team, averaging 12 points per game. After missing parts of the previous few seasons due to injury, Butler had a clean bill of health in 2011-12. He was able to play in 63 of the team's 66 games.

The Clippers also added guard Chauncey Billups, a 15-year veteran, and former NBA champion with the Detroit Pistons. After averaging almost 18 points per game to start the year, and forming a terrific backcourt with Chris Paul, Billups tore

Caron Butler was another key player on the 2011-12 Clippers. After nine seasons and four trips to the playoffs, Butler was a great

his Achilles tendon and missed the rest of the season.

After Billups' injury, Randy Foye joined the Clippers' regular starting lineup and provided solid scoring, especially from behind the three-point line. During one key late-

Great Track Record
From 2003-2009, Chauncey Billups played in seven straight Conference Finals—six with the Pistons and one with the Nuggets.

season win in Dallas, Foye hit eight three-pointers—only four short of the NBA record!

Paul and Billups set their defense against the Lakers.

DeAndre Jordan tangles with Boris Diaw in the lane.

the 2011-12 Clippers. He averaged more than 13 points per game off the bench.

The Clippers began the year on a tear, winning 15 of their first 22. With wins over the Heat, Thunder, and the Lakers, the Clippers had every reason to feel like a team that could compete with the NBA's best.

The Clippers cooled down after their hot start and lost 14 of their next 25. Even so, the team was still in the playoff hunt, and few people realistically thought the team would miss out on the postseason.

With the playoffs in sight, the Clippers looked to add depth to

Mo Williams had been a starting point guard for most of his career, but took on a "super-sub" role for their roster during the season. They added another power forward who had been chosen first overall in the NBA Draft, Kenyon Martin. Martin had signed with a Chinese team during the NBA lockout and chose to join the Clippers when he came back home. In March, they also made a trade to acquire Nick Young. Young could be described as "instant offense" off the bench, with deadly three-point aim and absolutely no fear about taking a big shot.

Strengthened by their new additions, and the return of talented, young guard Eric Bledsoe from an injury, the Clippers ended the season by winning 14 of their last 19 games. The team finished with a 40-26 record, good for second place in the Pacific Division. The Lakers came

in first, but only had one more win than the Clippers. If L.A. was still the Lakers' town, the gap was definitely closing.

Nick Young provided scoring off the bench for the 2011-12 Clippers.

39

Record Comeback

By erasing a 21-point deficit after three quarters, the Clippers tied the NBA play-off record for the largest fourth-quarter comeback.

For only the fifth time since the team had moved to California in 1978, the Clippers had earned a place in the NBA Playoffs. Their first round opponent: the Memphis Grizzlies.

The Grizzlies built an 18-point lead in the first quarter of Game 1 and didn't let up. With about two minutes left in the third, the lead was up to 27. Chris Paul had looked rusty. Blake Griffin hadn't made any impact on the boards. And Caron Butler broke his hand and had to leave the game.

Clippers fans watching on television hoped this first game wasn't a sign of things to come, and most people paying attention assumed the fourth quarter was a lost cause.

What happened in the game's final eight minutes for the team from L.A. sounds like it came straight out of a Hollywood movie studio.

As the team huddled up during

The Grizzlies looked like they were in total control of Game 1.

a timeout with eight minutes left to play, they found themselves down 95-71. They walked back out onto the court hoping to end this horrible night with some good play down the stretch.

And then, one after the other, the Clippers started making good plays. A lot of them…

Reggie Evans got fouled making a layup. Missed the free throw… Rebounded by Griffin… Griffin scored. 95-75.

Zach Randolph lost the ball out of bounds… Chris Paul hit a jumper. 95-77.

Randolph missed a shot. Nick Young rebounded, took a three-pointer. Missed. Rebounded by Eric

Reggie Evans maneuvers around the Grizzlies' Dante Cunningham.

Bledsoe. Bledsoe hit an 18-footer. Timeout Memphis. 95-79, 6:30 left to play.

Rudy Gay missed a jumper… Reggie Evans rebounded… Eric

Blake Griffin lays one in against the Grizzlies.

He's in the Zone!

During the Clippers' comeback in Game 1 against the Grizzlies, Nick Young hit three three-pointers in under a minute.

Bledsoe hit a three… Grizzlies guard Mike Conley was fouled… Missed one of his two free throws… Layup by Blake Griffin. 96-84.

For more than two minutes, neither team scored. Then…

Chris Paul drove, spotted Nick Young in the left corner… Young put up a three-pointer. Swish! 96-87.

O.J. Mayo missed a jumper… Paul got the rebound, dribbled down the court, spotted Young in the right corner… Young put up another three. Swish again! 96-90.

Conley missed a three-pointer… Reggie Evans grabbed the rebound, passed to Paul… Paul saw Young in the right corner again… Young shot again. Bingo! 96-93.

A minute later, the Clippers took the lead on a Reggie Evans layup, and sealed the amazing victory with two Chris Paul free throws with 23 seconds left.

"I don't think I've been part of a game like that, ever," Griffin said. "It was unbelievable."

The Game 1 comeback against the Grizzlies will probably be remembered as the greatest moment in Clippers' history—at least until the team makes a run at an NBA championship.

The Clippers lost Game 2 in Memphis by seven points, but rallied—barely—to win Game 3 by a single point, 87-86.

Then, the Clippers won Game 4 in overtime, behind 30 points by Blake Griffin.

One win away from advancing to the next round, the Clippers lost Game 5 by 12.

To avoid having to play a seventh and deciding game on the road, the Clippers would need to win Game 6 at home. This time, though, the Grizzlies would make the fourth

Kenyon Martin, along with other bench players, helped to clinch the series.

quarter comeback, winning by two and sending the series to Memphis for Game 7.

Blake Griffin had one of his worst games of the year in Game 7, due to a knee injury. So, it was a good thing for the Clippers that their bench had one of the best games of its season.

Nick Young had 13 points, Kenyon Martin finished with 11, and Eric Bledsoe had eight. The Clippers won the game 82-72 to clinch the series.

Next up were the San Antonio Spurs. For all of the youth, athleticism, and potential the Clippers had, the Spurs had a veteran core that had

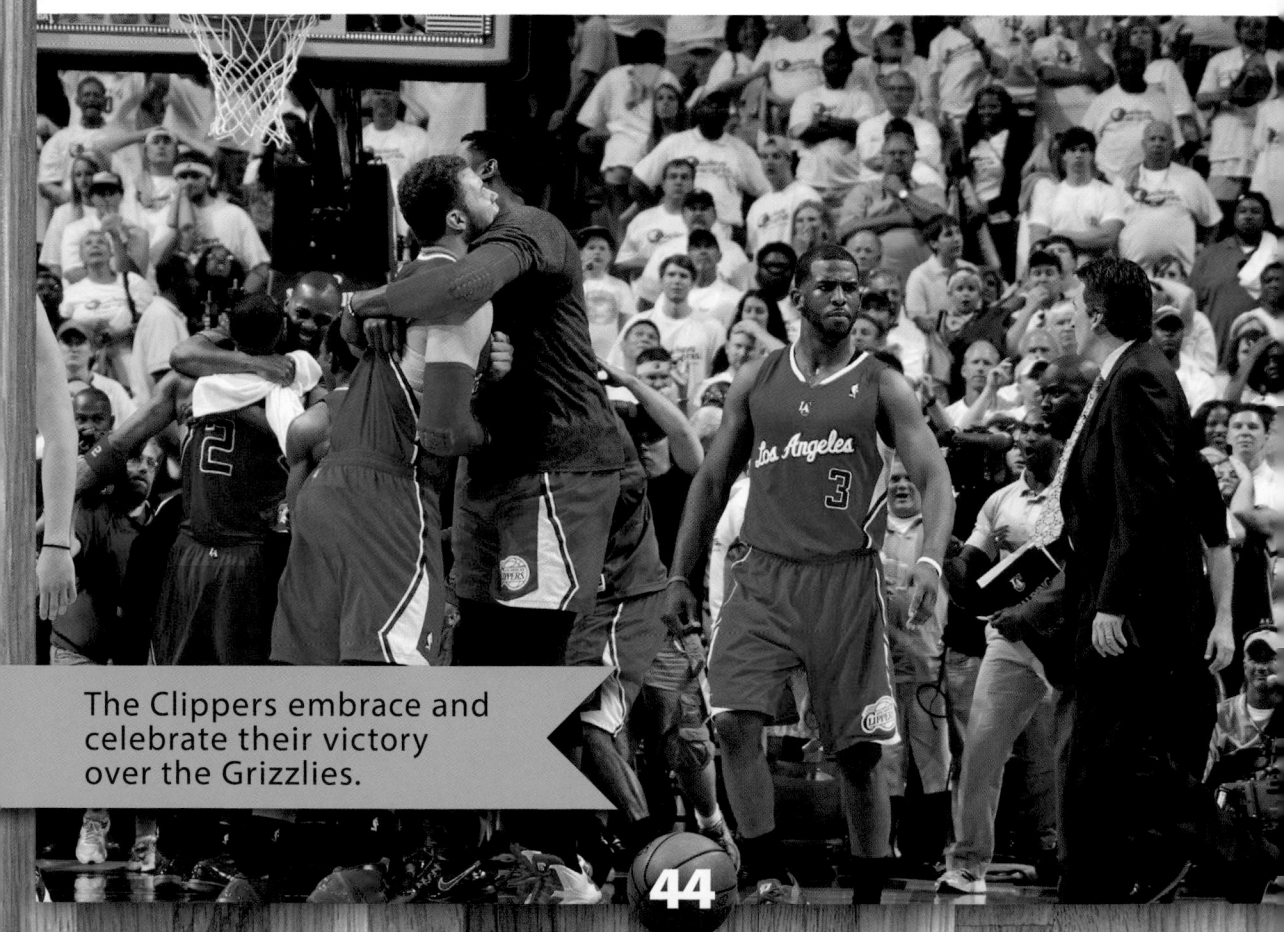

The Clippers embrace and celebrate their victory over the Grizzlies.

earned three NBA titles together. The Spurs also had the Western Conference's best record in 2011-12.

Unfortunately for the Clippers, their series with the Spurs was over fairly quickly. The Spurs blew the Clippers out in the first two games in San Antonio. In Game 3 in L.A., the Clippers brought a lead into the second half, but got crushed in the third quarter, 26-8, and lost by 10. The final game in the series was close, but the Clippers fell by three points, 102-99, and their season was over.

Clippers fans were thrilled with the 2011-12 season, even if the ending wasn't quite what they would have wanted.

Looking ahead to next year and beyond, the Clippers will need to keep improving in order to make progress in their unofficial "Battle

Blake Griffin and his teammates met their match against the Spurs.

for L.A." with the Lakers. While there will surely be new players wearing the red and white with each passing season, the real test for the Clippers is going to be keeping the star players they already have.

Assuming they stay injury-free, with Blake Griffin and Chris Paul on the roster, the team is likely to compete for a playoff spot almost every season. But, Chris Paul's contract will expire after the 2012-13 season, and Blake Griffin's will expire the year after that.

With at least one more season of "Lob City" assured, the immediate future looks bright for the Clippers. But, how the team handles those two contract situations will likely determine whether the Battle for L.A. will continue for the foreseeable future… or whether the Clippers yet again become "L.A.'s Other Team."

Jamal Crawford and Grant Hill, both pictured here, will join the Clippers in 2012-13.

The future looks bright for the Clippers with Paul and Griffin on the roster.